This Journal Belongs to: _____

SMART Goals

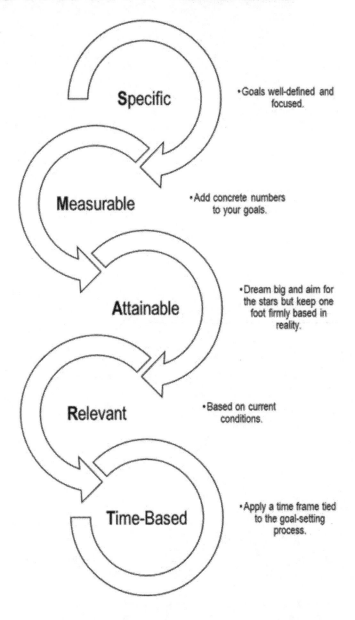

Specific — •Goals well-defined and focused.

Measurable — •Add concrete numbers to your goals.

Attainable — •Dream big and aim for the stars but keep one foot firmly based in reality.

Relevant — •Based on current conditions.

Time-Based — •Apply a time frame tied to the goal-setting process.

Vision Board

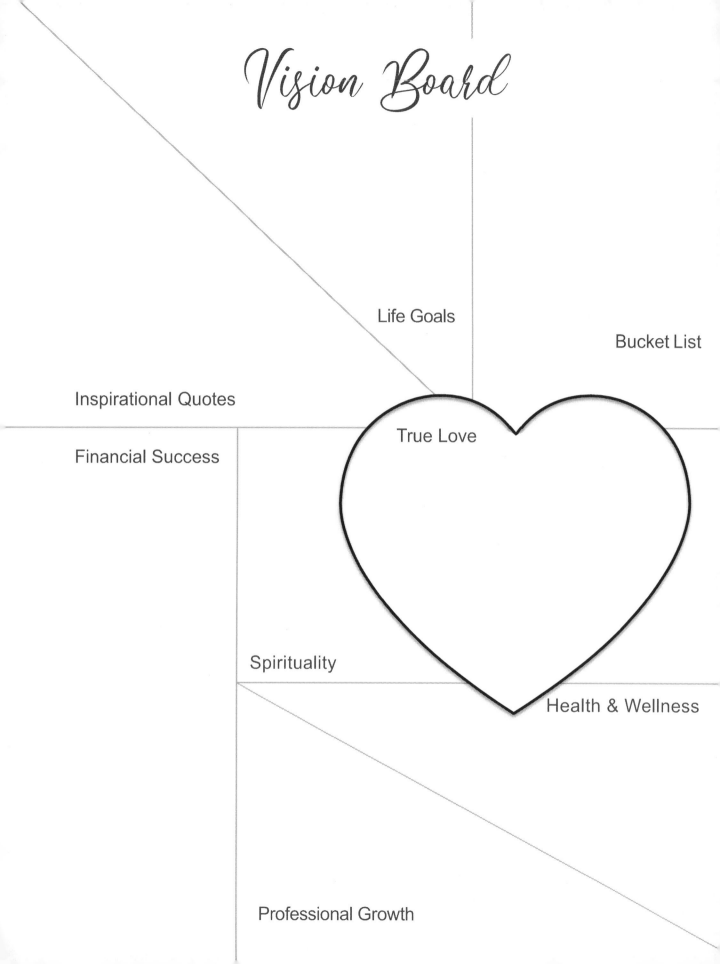

Life Goals

Bucket List

Inspirational Quotes

True Love

Financial Success

Spirituality

Health & Wellness

Professional Growth

Manifest Objective:

_____
_____
_____
_____
_____
_____

Steps to Success

_____
_____
_____
_____
_____
_____
_____
_____
_____
_____
_____
_____

Next New Moon:

_____

Important Dates

_____
_____
_____
_____
_____
_____
_____

Resources

_____
_____
_____
_____
_____
_____

Notes and Reflections

VISION
PLAN
ACTION
SUCCESS

_____
_____
_____
_____
_____

Monthly Planner

MONDAY	TUESDAY	WEDNESDAY	THURSDAY	FRIDAY	SATURDAY	SUNDAY

Weekly Action Plan

WEEK OF

MONDAY	
TASK	COMPLETED?

TUESDAY	
TASK	COMPLETED?

WEDNESDAY	
TASK	COMPLETED?

THURSDAY	
TASK	COMPLETED?

FRIDAY	
TASK	COMPLETED?

WEEKEND	
TASK	COMPLETED?

Weekly Action Plan

———————— WEEK OF ————————

MONDAY	
TASK	COMPLETED?

TUESDAY	
TASK	COMPLETED?

WEDNESDAY	
TASK	COMPLETED?

THURSDAY	
TASK	COMPLETED?

FRIDAY	
TASK	COMPLETED?

WEEKEND	
TASK	COMPLETED?

Weekly Action Plan

WEEK OF

MONDAY

TASK	COMPLETED?

TUESDAY

TASK	COMPLETED?

WEDNESDAY

TASK	COMPLETED?

THURSDAY

TASK	COMPLETED?

FRIDAY

TASK	COMPLETED?

WEEKEND

TASK	COMPLETED?

Weekly Action Plan

──────────── WEEK OF ────────────

MONDAY	
TASK	COMPLETED?

TUESDAY	
TASK	COMPLETED?

WEDNESDAY	
TASK	COMPLETED?

THURSDAY	
TASK	COMPLETED?

FRIDAY	
TASK	COMPLETED?

WEEKEND	
TASK	COMPLETED?

Weekly Action Plan

WEEK OF

MONDAY

TASK	COMPLETED?

TUESDAY

TASK	COMPLETED?

WEDNESDAY

TASK	COMPLETED?

THURSDAY

TASK	COMPLETED?

FRIDAY

TASK	COMPLETED?

WEEKEND

TASK	COMPLETED?

Manifest Journal

Date: _____

I am beautiful and worthy of every truly beautiful thing.

_____

_____

_____

_____

_____

_____

_____

_____

_____

_____

_____

_____

_____

_____

_____

_____

Manifest Journal

Date: _____

I respect my need to rest and recharge.

_____

_____

_____

_____

_____

_____

_____

_____

_____

_____

_____

_____

_____

_____

_____

_____

_____

_____

Vision Board

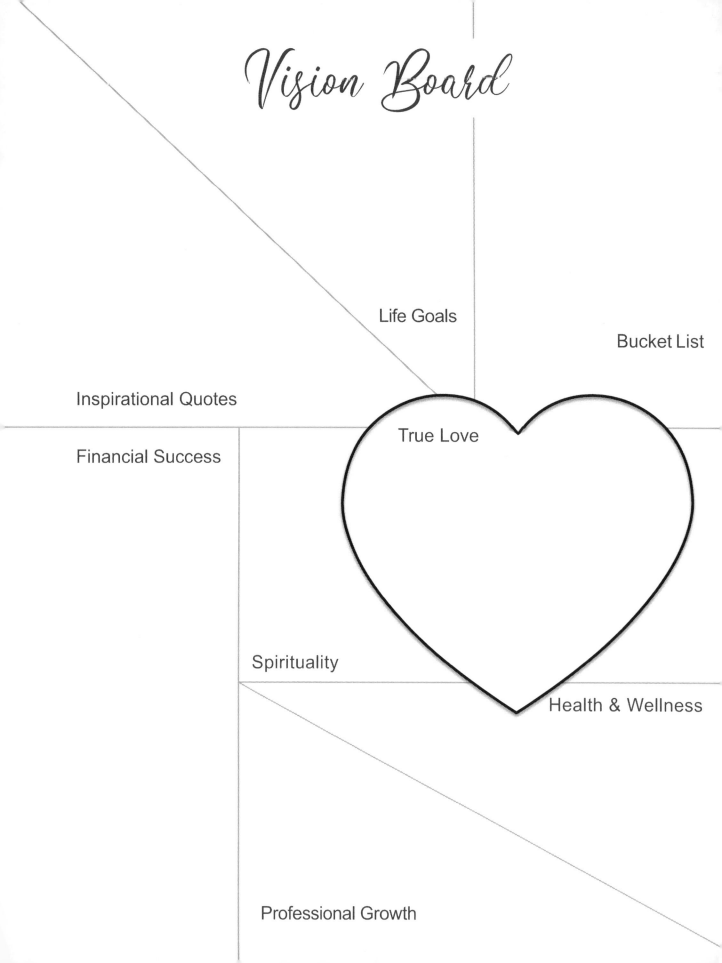

Life Goals

Bucket List

Inspirational Quotes

True Love

Financial Success

Spirituality

Health & Wellness

Professional Growth

Manifest Objective:

_____

_____

_____

_____

_____

Steps to Success

_____

_____

_____

_____

_____

_____

_____

_____

_____

_____

_____

_____

Notes and Reflections

Next New Moon:

_____

Important Dates

_____

_____

_____

_____

_____

Resources

_____

_____

_____

_____

VISION
PLAN
ACTION
SUCCESS

_____

_____

_____

_____

Monthly Planner

MONDAY	TUESDAY	WEDNESDAY	THURSDAY	FRIDAY	SATURDAY	SUNDAY

Weekly Action Plan

WEEK OF

MONDAY	
TASK	COMPLETED?

TUESDAY	
TASK	COMPLETED?

WEDNESDAY	
TASK	COMPLETED?

THURSDAY	
TASK	COMPLETED?

FRIDAY	
TASK	COMPLETED?

WEEKEND	
TASK	COMPLETED?

Weekly Action Plan

WEEK OF

MONDAY	
TASK	COMPLETED?

TUESDAY	
TASK	COMPLETED?

WEDNESDAY	
TASK	COMPLETED?

THURSDAY	
TASK	COMPLETED?

FRIDAY	
TASK	COMPLETED?

WEEKEND	
TASK	COMPLETED?

Weekly Action Plan

WEEK OF

MONDAY

TASK	COMPLETED?

TUESDAY

TASK	COMPLETED?

WEDNESDAY

TASK	COMPLETED?

THURSDAY

TASK	COMPLETED?

FRIDAY

TASK	COMPLETED?

WEEKEND

TASK	COMPLETED?

Weekly Action Plan

WEEK OF

MONDAY	
TASK	COMPLETED?

TUESDAY	
TASK	COMPLETED?

WEDNESDAY	
TASK	COMPLETED?

THURSDAY	
TASK	COMPLETED?

FRIDAY	
TASK	COMPLETED?

WEEKEND	
TASK	COMPLETED?

Weekly Action Plan

WEEK OF

MONDAY

TASK	COMPLETED?

TUESDAY

TASK	COMPLETED?

WEDNESDAY

TASK	COMPLETED?

THURSDAY

TASK	COMPLETED?

FRIDAY

TASK	COMPLETED?

WEEKEND

TASK	COMPLETED?

Manifest Journal

I have the power to create my own reality.

_____

_____

_____

_____

_____

_____

_____

_____

_____

_____

_____

_____

_____

_____

_____

_____

Manifest Journal

I am the architect of my own success.

_____

_____

_____

_____

_____

_____

_____

_____

_____

_____

_____

_____

_____

_____

_____

_____

_____

_____

_____

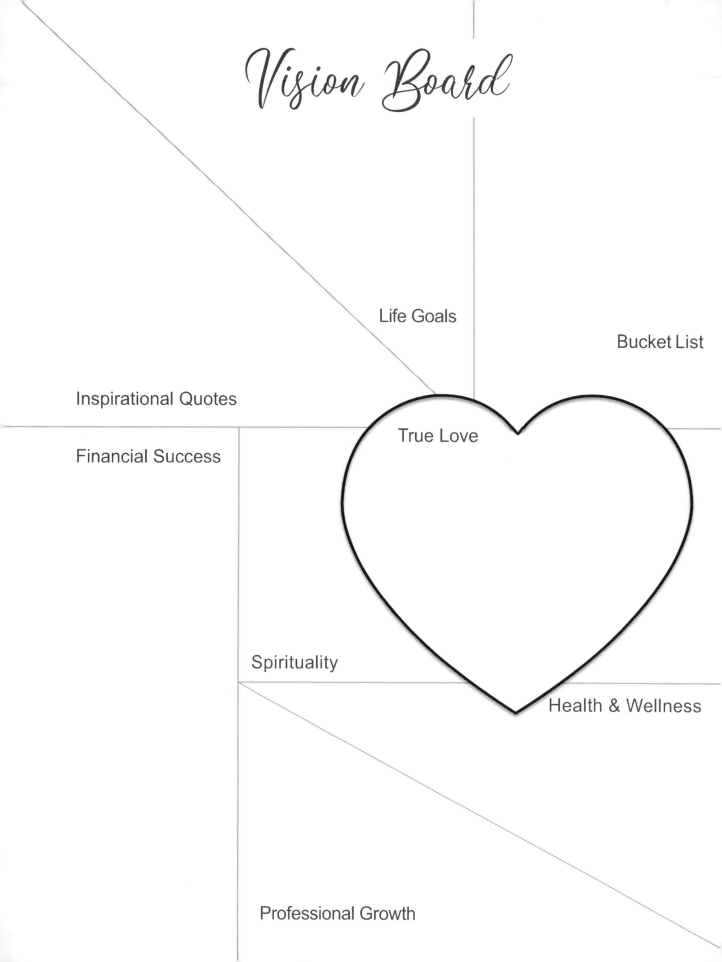

Vision Board

Life Goals

Bucket List

Inspirational Quotes

True Love

Financial Success

Spirituality

Health & Wellness

Professional Growth

Manifest Objective:

_____
_____
_____
_____
_____

Steps to Success

_____
_____
_____
_____
_____
_____
_____
_____
_____

Notes and Reflections

Next New Moon:

_____

Important Dates

_____
_____
_____
_____
_____

Resources

_____
_____
_____
_____

VISION
PLAN
ACTION
SUCCESS

_____
_____
_____
_____
_____

Monthly Planner

MONTH / YEAR

MONDAY	TUESDAY	WEDNESDAY	THURSDAY	FRIDAY	SATURDAY	SUNDAY

Weekly Action Plan

WEEK OF

MONDAY	
TASK	COMPLETED?

TUESDAY	
TASK	COMPLETED?

WEDNESDAY	
TASK	COMPLETED?

THURSDAY	
TASK	COMPLETED?

FRIDAY	
TASK	COMPLETED?

WEEKEND	
TASK	COMPLETED?

Weekly Action Plan

WEEK OF

MONDAY

TASK	COMPLETED?

TUESDAY

TASK	COMPLETED?

WEDNESDAY

TASK	COMPLETED?

THURSDAY

TASK	COMPLETED?

FRIDAY

TASK	COMPLETED?

WEEKEND

TASK	COMPLETED?

Weekly Action Plan

WEEK OF

MONDAY

TASK	COMPLETED?

TUESDAY

TASK	COMPLETED?

WEDNESDAY

TASK	COMPLETED?

THURSDAY

TASK	COMPLETED?

FRIDAY

TASK	COMPLETED?

WEEKEND

TASK	COMPLETED?

Weekly Action Plan

WEEK OF

MONDAY

TASK	COMPLETED?

TUESDAY

TASK	COMPLETED?

WEDNESDAY

TASK	COMPLETED?

THURSDAY

TASK	COMPLETED?

FRIDAY

TASK	COMPLETED?

WEEKEND

TASK	COMPLETED?

Weekly Action Plan

WEEK OF

MONDAY

TASK	COMPLETED?

TUESDAY

TASK	COMPLETED?

WEDNESDAY

TASK	COMPLETED?

THURSDAY

TASK	COMPLETED?

FRIDAY

TASK	COMPLETED?

WEEKEND

TASK	COMPLETED?

Manifest Journal

I am allowed to be myself and show the world who I am.

Manifest Journal

I honor my commitment to take care of myself.

_____

_____

_____

_____

_____

_____

_____

_____

_____

_____

_____

_____

_____

_____

_____

_____

_____

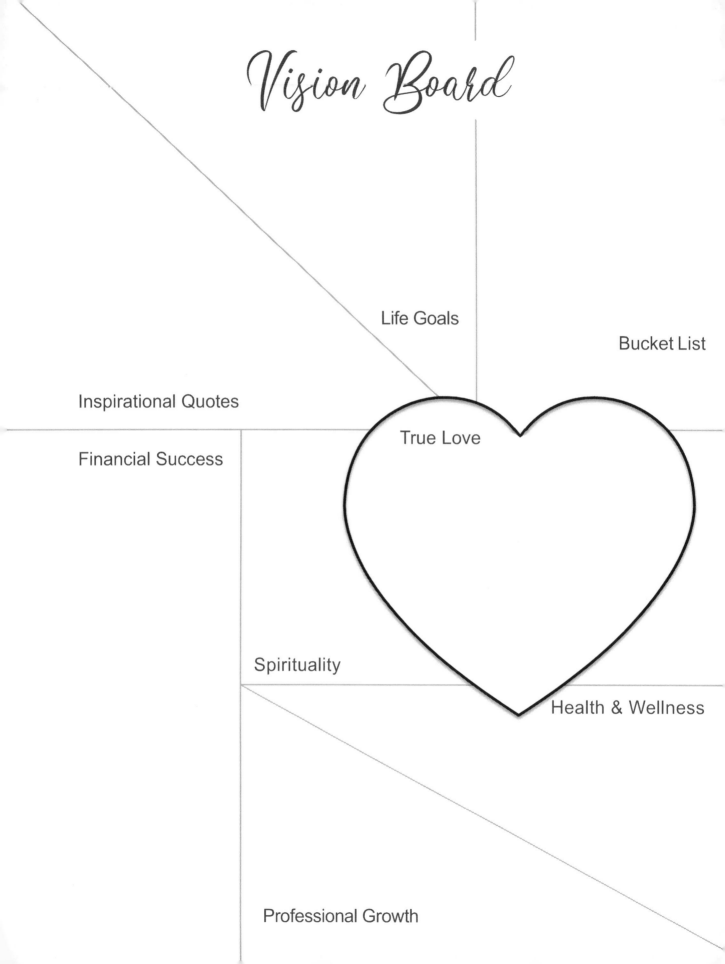

Vision Board

Life Goals

Bucket List

Inspirational Quotes

Financial Success

True Love

Spirituality

Health & Wellness

Professional Growth

Manifest Objective:

_____
_____
_____
_____
_____

Steps to Success

_____
_____
_____
_____
_____
_____
_____
_____
_____
_____

Notes and Reflections

Next New Moon:

_____

Important Dates

_____
_____
_____
_____
_____
_____

Resources

_____
_____
_____
_____
_____

VISION
PLAN
ACTION
SUCCESS

_____
_____
_____
_____

Monthly Planner

MONTH / YEAR

MONDAY	TUESDAY	WEDNESDAY	THURSDAY	FRIDAY	SATURDAY	SUNDAY

Weekly Action Plan

WEEK OF

MONDAY

TASK	COMPLETED?

TUESDAY

TASK	COMPLETED?

WEDNESDAY

TASK	COMPLETED?

THURSDAY

TASK	COMPLETED?

FRIDAY

TASK	COMPLETED?

WEEKEND

TASK	COMPLETED?

Weekly Action Plan

WEEK OF

MONDAY	
TASK	COMPLETED?

TUESDAY	
TASK	COMPLETED?

WEDNESDAY	
TASK	COMPLETED?

THURSDAY	
TASK	COMPLETED?

FRIDAY	
TASK	COMPLETED?

WEEKEND	
TASK	COMPLETED?

Weekly Action Plan

WEEK OF

MONDAY	
TASK	COMPLETED?

TUESDAY	
TASK	COMPLETED?

WEDNESDAY	
TASK	COMPLETED?

THURSDAY	
TASK	COMPLETED?

FRIDAY	
TASK	COMPLETED?

WEEKEND	
TASK	COMPLETED?

Weekly Action Plan

WEEK OF

MONDAY

TASK	COMPLETED?

TUESDAY

TASK	COMPLETED?

WEDNESDAY

TASK	COMPLETED?

THURSDAY

TASK	COMPLETED?

FRIDAY

TASK	COMPLETED?

WEEKEND

TASK	COMPLETED?

Weekly Action Plan

WEEK OF

MONDAY

TASK	COMPLETED?

TUESDAY

TASK	COMPLETED?

WEDNESDAY

TASK	COMPLETED?

THURSDAY

TASK	COMPLETED?

FRIDAY

TASK	COMPLETED?

WEEKEND

TASK	COMPLETED?

Manifest Journal

I am becoming a better version of myself each day.

Manifest Journal

Date: _____

I am committed to accomplishing my goals, regardless of any mistakes I make along the way.

_____

_____

_____

_____

_____

_____

_____

_____

_____

_____

_____

_____

_____

_____

_____

_____

_____

_____

_____

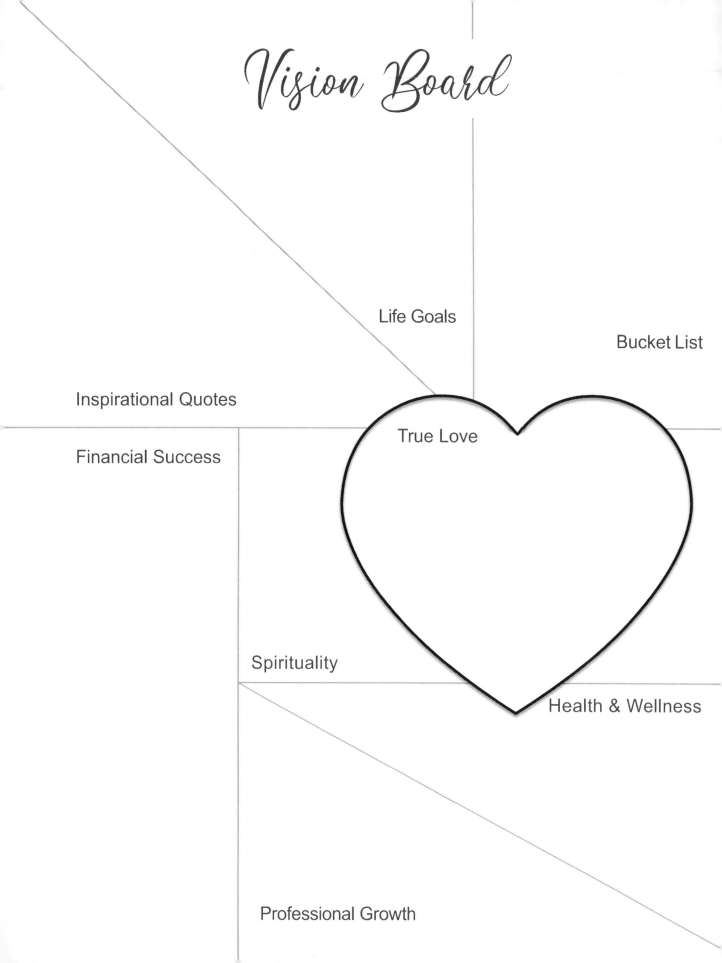

Vision Board

Life Goals

Bucket List

Inspirational Quotes

True Love

Financial Success

Spirituality

Health & Wellness

Professional Growth

Manifest Objective:

_____
_____
_____
_____
_____

Steps to Success

_____
_____
_____
_____
_____
_____
_____
_____
_____
_____
_____

Next New Moon:

_____

Important Dates

_____
_____
_____
_____
_____
_____

Resources

_____
_____
_____
_____
_____

Notes and Reflections

_____
_____
_____
_____
_____

Monthly Planner

MONDAY	TUESDAY	WEDNESDAY	THURSDAY	FRIDAY	SATURDAY	SUNDAY

Weekly Action Plan

WEEK OF

MONDAY	
TASK	COMPLETED?

TUESDAY	
TASK	COMPLETED?

WEDNESDAY	
TASK	COMPLETED?

THURSDAY	
TASK	COMPLETED?

FRIDAY	
TASK	COMPLETED?

WEEKEND	
TASK	COMPLETED?

Weekly Action Plan

WEEK OF

MONDAY

TASK	COMPLETED?

TUESDAY

TASK	COMPLETED?

WEDNESDAY

TASK	COMPLETED?

THURSDAY

TASK	COMPLETED?

FRIDAY

TASK	COMPLETED?

WEEKEND

TASK	COMPLETED?

Weekly Action Plan

WEEK OF

MONDAY	
TASK	COMPLETED?

TUESDAY	
TASK	COMPLETED?

WEDNESDAY	
TASK	COMPLETED?

THURSDAY	
TASK	COMPLETED?

FRIDAY	
TASK	COMPLETED?

WEEKEND	
TASK	COMPLETED?

Weekly Action Plan

WEEK OF

MONDAY	
TASK	COMPLETED?

TUESDAY	
TASK	COMPLETED?

WEDNESDAY	
TASK	COMPLETED?

THURSDAY	
TASK	COMPLETED?

FRIDAY	
TASK	COMPLETED?

WEEKEND	
TASK	COMPLETED?

Weekly Action Plan

WEEK OF

MONDAY

TASK	COMPLETED?

TUESDAY

TASK	COMPLETED?

WEDNESDAY

TASK	COMPLETED?

THURSDAY

TASK	COMPLETED?

FRIDAY

TASK	COMPLETED?

WEEKEND

TASK	COMPLETED?

Manifest Journal

Date: _____

I am uniquely gifted and powerful.

_____

_____

_____

_____

_____

_____

_____

_____

_____

_____

_____

_____

_____

_____

_____

_____

_____

_____

Manifest Journal

Date: _____

I am deliberate, and afraid of nothing.

_____

_____

_____

_____

_____

_____

_____

_____

_____

_____

_____

_____

_____

_____

_____

_____

_____

_____

_____

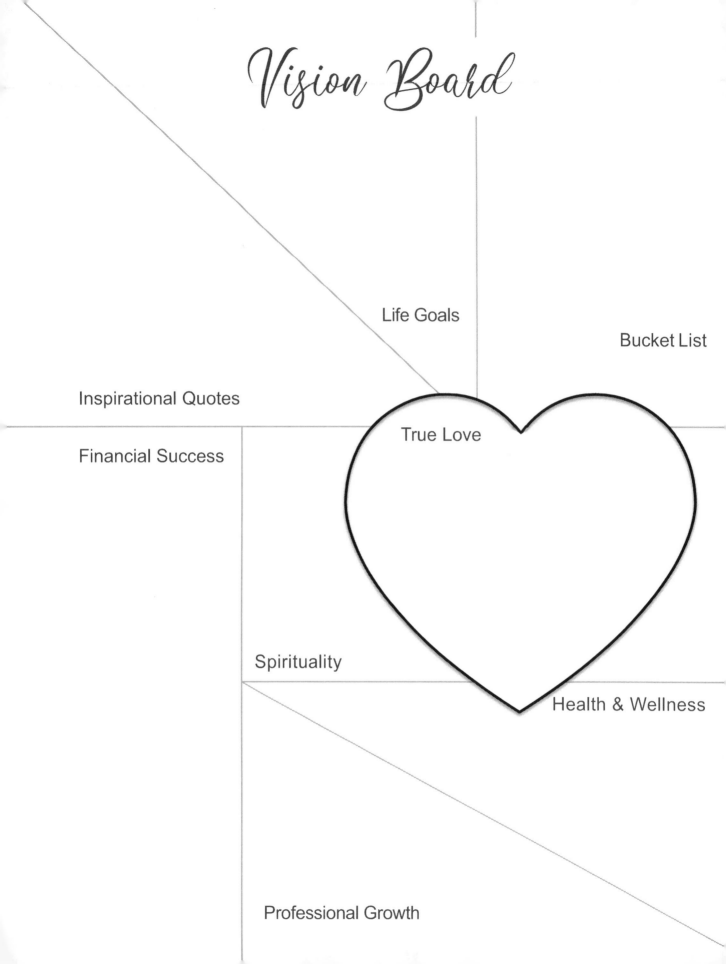

Vision Board

Life Goals

Bucket List

Inspirational Quotes

True Love

Financial Success

Spirituality

Health & Wellness

Professional Growth

Manifest Objective:

_____
_____
_____
_____
_____

Steps to Success

_____
_____
_____
_____
_____
_____
_____
_____
_____
_____
_____

Notes and Reflections

Next New Moon:

_____

Important Dates

_____
_____
_____
_____
_____

Resources

_____
_____
_____
_____

VISION
PLAN
ACTION
SUCCESS

_____
_____
_____
_____

Monthly Planner

MONDAY	TUESDAY	WEDNESDAY	THURSDAY	FRIDAY	SATURDAY	SUNDAY

Weekly Action Plan

WEEK OF

MONDAY

TASK	COMPLETED?

TUESDAY

TASK	COMPLETED?

WEDNESDAY

TASK	COMPLETED?

THURSDAY

TASK	COMPLETED?

FRIDAY

TASK	COMPLETED?

WEEKEND

TASK	COMPLETED?

Weekly Action Plan

WEEK OF

MONDAY

TASK	COMPLETED?

TUESDAY

TASK	COMPLETED?

WEDNESDAY

TASK	COMPLETED?

THURSDAY

TASK	COMPLETED?

FRIDAY

TASK	COMPLETED?

WEEKEND

TASK	COMPLETED?

Weekly Action Plan

WEEK OF

MONDAY	
TASK	COMPLETED?

TUESDAY	
TASK	COMPLETED?

WEDNESDAY	
TASK	COMPLETED?

THURSDAY	
TASK	COMPLETED?

FRIDAY	
TASK	COMPLETED?

WEEKEND	
TASK	COMPLETED?

Weekly Action Plan

───── WEEK OF ─────

| |
| |

MONDAY

TASK	COMPLETED?

TUESDAY

TASK	COMPLETED?

WEDNESDAY

TASK	COMPLETED?

THURSDAY

TASK	COMPLETED?

FRIDAY

TASK	COMPLETED?

WEEKEND

TASK	COMPLETED?

Weekly Action Plan

WEEK OF

MONDAY	
TASK	COMPLETED?

TUESDAY	
TASK	COMPLETED?

WEDNESDAY	
TASK	COMPLETED?

THURSDAY	
TASK	COMPLETED?

FRIDAY	
TASK	COMPLETED?

WEEKEND	
TASK	COMPLETED?

Manifest Journal

Date: _____

Today is the future that I created yesterday.

_____

_____

_____

_____

_____

_____

_____

_____

_____

_____

_____

_____

_____

_____

_____

_____

Manifest Journal

Date: _____

I am committed to my own success.

_____

_____

_____

_____

_____

_____

_____

_____

_____

_____

_____

_____

_____

_____

_____

_____

_____

_____

_____

_____

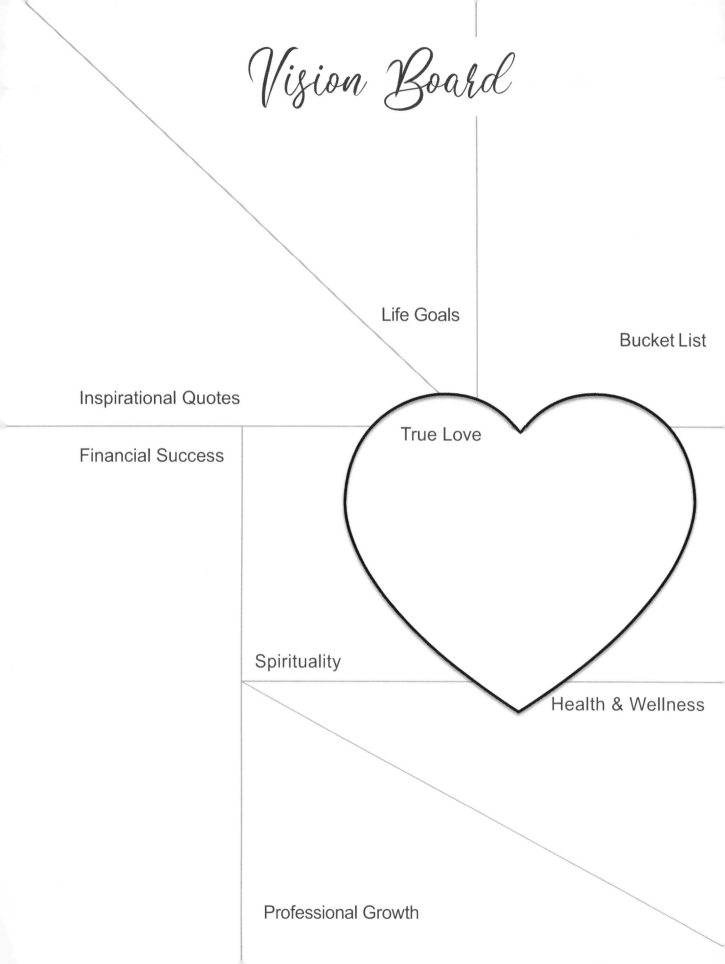

Vision Board

Life Goals

Bucket List

Inspirational Quotes

Financial Success

True Love

Spirituality

Health & Wellness

Professional Growth

Manifest Objective:

_____
_____
_____
_____
_____

Steps to Success

_____
_____
_____
_____
_____
_____
_____
_____
_____
_____
_____
_____

Notes and Reflections

Next New Moon:

_____

Important Dates

_____
_____
_____
_____
_____

Resources

_____
_____
_____
_____
_____

VISION
PLAN
ACTION
SUCCESS

_____
_____
_____
_____

Monthly Planner

MONDAY	TUESDAY	WEDNESDAY	THURSDAY	FRIDAY	SATURDAY	SUNDAY

Weekly Action Plan

——————— WEEK OF ———————

MONDAY	
TASK	COMPLETED?

TUESDAY	
TASK	COMPLETED?

WEDNESDAY	
TASK	COMPLETED?

THURSDAY	
TASK	COMPLETED?

FRIDAY	
TASK	COMPLETED?

WEEKEND	
TASK	COMPLETED?

Weekly Action Plan

WEEK OF

MONDAY

TASK	COMPLETED?

TUESDAY

TASK	COMPLETED?

WEDNESDAY

TASK	COMPLETED?

THURSDAY

TASK	COMPLETED?

FRIDAY

TASK	COMPLETED?

WEEKEND

TASK	COMPLETED?

Weekly Action Plan

WEEK OF

MONDAY

TASK	COMPLETED?

TUESDAY

TASK	COMPLETED?

WEDNESDAY

TASK	COMPLETED?

THURSDAY

TASK	COMPLETED?

FRIDAY

TASK	COMPLETED?

WEEKEND

TASK	COMPLETED?

Weekly Action Plan

WEEK OF

MONDAY	
TASK	COMPLETED?

TUESDAY	
TASK	COMPLETED?

WEDNESDAY	
TASK	COMPLETED?

THURSDAY	
TASK	COMPLETED?

FRIDAY	
TASK	COMPLETED?

WEEKEND	
TASK	COMPLETED?

Weekly Action Plan

WEEK OF

MONDAY

TASK	COMPLETED?

TUESDAY

TASK	COMPLETED?

WEDNESDAY

TASK	COMPLETED?

THURSDAY

TASK	COMPLETED?

FRIDAY

TASK	COMPLETED?

WEEKEND

TASK	COMPLETED?

Date: _____

I possess the qualities needed to be extremely successful.

_____

_____

_____

_____

_____

_____

_____

_____

_____

_____

_____

_____

_____

_____

_____

_____

Manifest Journal

Date: _____

I take my goals seriously

_____

_____

_____

_____

_____

_____

_____

_____

_____

_____

_____

_____

_____

_____

_____

_____

_____

_____

_____

Vision Board

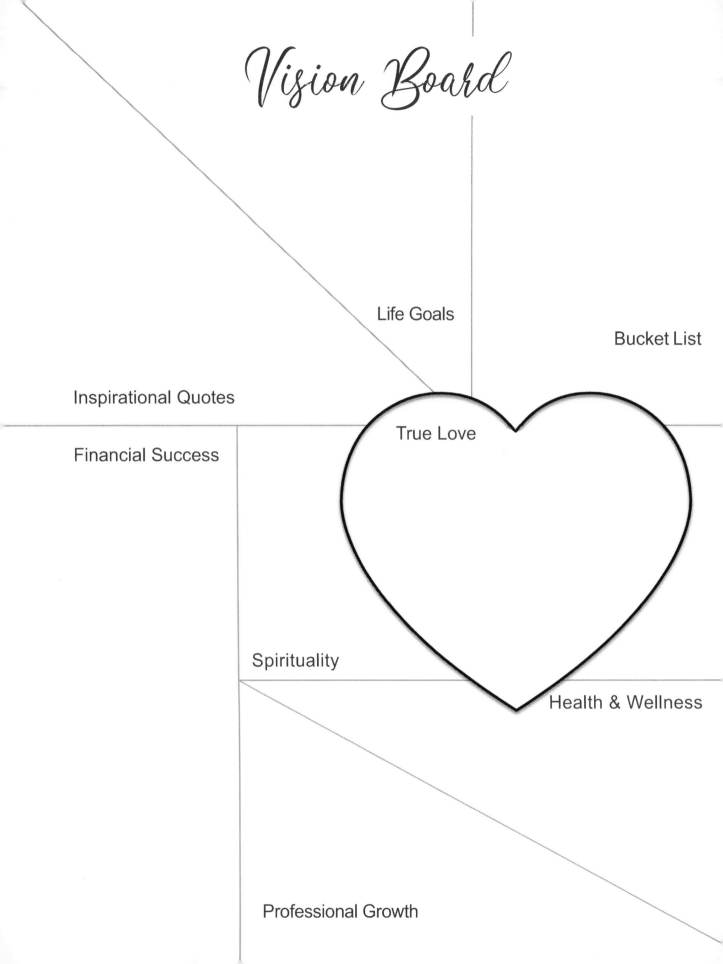

Life Goals

Bucket List

Inspirational Quotes

True Love

Financial Success

Spirituality

Health & Wellness

Professional Growth

Manifest Objective:

_____

_____

_____

_____

_____

Steps to Success

_____

_____

_____

_____

_____

_____

_____

_____

_____

_____

_____

Next New Moon:

_____

Important Dates

_____

_____

_____

_____

_____

Resources

_____

_____

_____

_____

_____

VISION
PLAN
ACTION
SUCCESS

Notes and Reflections

_____

_____

_____

_____

_____

Monthly Planner

MONDAY	TUESDAY	WEDNESDAY	THURSDAY	FRIDAY	SATURDAY	SUNDAY

Weekly Action Plan

———————— WEEK OF ————————

MONDAY

TASK	COMPLETED?

TUESDAY

TASK	COMPLETED?

WEDNESDAY

TASK	COMPLETED?

THURSDAY

TASK	COMPLETED?

FRIDAY

TASK	COMPLETED?

WEEKEND

TASK	COMPLETED?

Weekly Action Plan

WEEK OF

MONDAY	
TASK	COMPLETED?

TUESDAY	
TASK	COMPLETED?

WEDNESDAY	
TASK	COMPLETED?

THURSDAY	
TASK	COMPLETED?

FRIDAY	
TASK	COMPLETED?

WEEKEND	
TASK	COMPLETED?

Weekly Action Plan

———— WEEK OF ————

MONDAY

TASK	COMPLETED?

TUESDAY

TASK	COMPLETED?

WEDNESDAY

TASK	COMPLETED?

THURSDAY

TASK	COMPLETED?

FRIDAY

TASK	COMPLETED?

WEEKEND

TASK	COMPLETED?

Weekly Action Plan

───────────── WEEK OF ─────────────

MONDAY		TUESDAY	
TASK	COMPLETED?	TASK	COMPLETED?

WEDNESDAY		THURSDAY	
TASK	COMPLETED?	TASK	COMPLETED?

FRIDAY		WEEKEND	
TASK	COMPLETED?	TASK	COMPLETED?

Weekly Action Plan

WEEK OF

MONDAY

TASK	COMPLETED?

TUESDAY

TASK	COMPLETED?

WEDNESDAY

TASK	COMPLETED?

THURSDAY

TASK	COMPLETED?

FRIDAY

TASK	COMPLETED?

WEEKEND

TASK	COMPLETED?

Manifest Journal

Date: _____

I release my need to compare myself to others.

_____

_____

_____

_____

_____

_____

_____

_____

_____

_____

_____

_____

_____

_____

_____

_____

I choose to take responsibility for my own life.

_____

_____

_____

_____

_____

_____

_____

_____

_____

_____

_____

_____

_____

_____

_____

_____

Vision Board

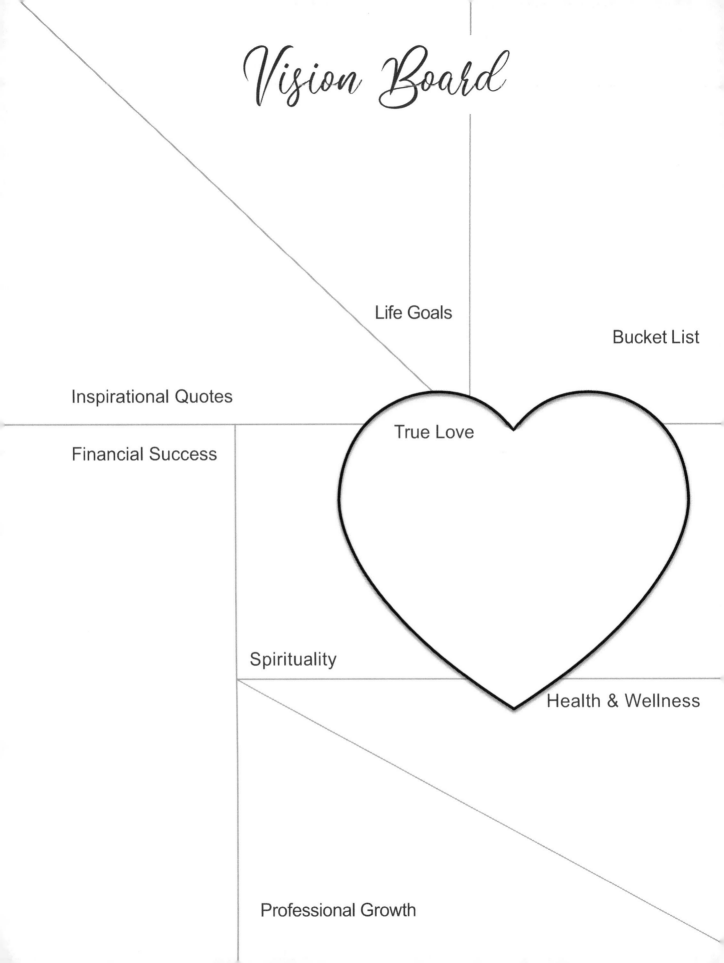

Life Goals

Bucket List

Inspirational Quotes

True Love

Financial Success

Spirituality

Health & Wellness

Professional Growth

Manifest Objective:

_____
_____
_____
_____
_____

Steps to Success

_____
_____
_____
_____
_____
_____
_____
_____
_____
_____

Next New Moon:

_____

Important Dates

_____
_____
_____
_____
_____
_____

Resources

_____
_____
_____
_____
_____

VISION
PLAN
ACTION
SUCCESS

Notes and Reflections

_____
_____
_____
_____

Monthly Planner

MONDAY	TUESDAY	WEDNESDAY	THURSDAY	FRIDAY	SATURDAY	SUNDAY

Weekly Action Plan

WEEK OF

MONDAY

TASK	COMPLETED?

TUESDAY

TASK	COMPLETED?

WEDNESDAY

TASK	COMPLETED?

THURSDAY

TASK	COMPLETED?

FRIDAY

TASK	COMPLETED?

WEEKEND

TASK	COMPLETED?

Weekly Action Plan

WEEK OF

MONDAY

TASK	COMPLETED?

TUESDAY

TASK	COMPLETED?

WEDNESDAY

TASK	COMPLETED?

THURSDAY

TASK	COMPLETED?

FRIDAY

TASK	COMPLETED?

WEEKEND

TASK	COMPLETED?

Weekly Action Plan

WEEK OF

MONDAY	
TASK	COMPLETED?

TUESDAY	
TASK	COMPLETED?

WEDNESDAY	
TASK	COMPLETED?

THURSDAY	
TASK	COMPLETED?

FRIDAY	
TASK	COMPLETED?

WEEKEND	
TASK	COMPLETED?

Weekly Action Plan

WEEK OF

MONDAY	
TASK	COMPLETED?

TUESDAY	
TASK	COMPLETED?

WEDNESDAY	
TASK	COMPLETED?

THURSDAY	
TASK	COMPLETED?

FRIDAY	
TASK	COMPLETED?

WEEKEND	
TASK	COMPLETED?

Weekly Action Plan

WEEK OF

MONDAY	
TASK	COMPLETED?

TUESDAY	
TASK	COMPLETED?

WEDNESDAY	
TASK	COMPLETED?

THURSDAY	
TASK	COMPLETED?

FRIDAY	
TASK	COMPLETED?

WEEKEND	
TASK	COMPLETED?

Manifest Journal

Date: _____

I believe in my own power.

_____

_____

_____

_____

_____

_____

_____

_____

_____

_____

_____

_____

_____

_____

_____

_____

_____

Date: _____

I love who I am.

_____

_____

_____

_____

_____

_____

_____

_____

_____

_____

_____

_____

_____

_____

_____

_____

_____

_____

_____

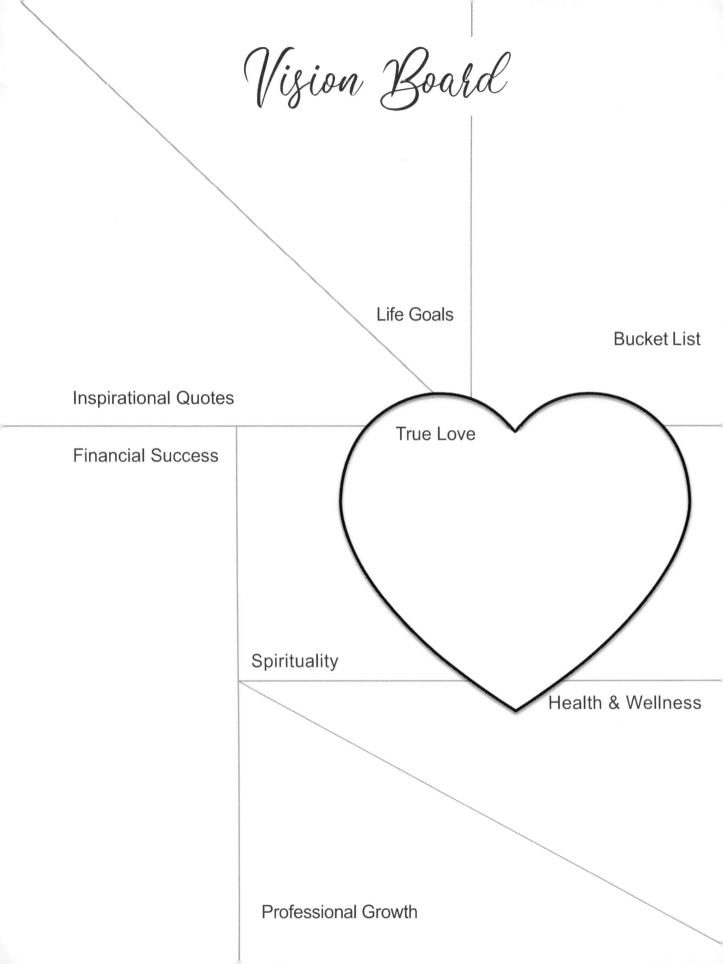

Vision Board

Life Goals

Bucket List

Inspirational Quotes

True Love

Financial Success

Spirituality

Health & Wellness

Professional Growth

Manifest Objective:

_____
_____
_____
_____
_____
_____

Steps to Success

_____
_____
_____
_____
_____
_____
_____
_____
_____
_____
_____
_____

Notes and Reflections

Next New Moon:

_____

Important Dates

_____
_____
_____
_____
_____
_____
_____

Resources

_____
_____
_____
_____
_____

VISION
PLAN
ACTION
SUCCESS

_____
_____
_____
_____
_____

Monthly Planner

MONTH / YEAR

MONDAY	TUESDAY	WEDNESDAY	THURSDAY	FRIDAY	SATURDAY	SUNDAY

Weekly Action Plan

WEEK OF

MONDAY

TASK	COMPLETED?

TUESDAY

TASK	COMPLETED?

WEDNESDAY

TASK	COMPLETED?

THURSDAY

TASK	COMPLETED?

FRIDAY

TASK	COMPLETED?

WEEKEND

TASK	COMPLETED?

Weekly Action Plan

WEEK OF

MONDAY	
TASK	COMPLETED?

TUESDAY	
TASK	COMPLETED?

WEDNESDAY	
TASK	COMPLETED?

THURSDAY	
TASK	COMPLETED?

FRIDAY	
TASK	COMPLETED?

WEEKEND	
TASK	COMPLETED?

Weekly Action Plan

—— WEEK OF ——

MONDAY	
TASK	COMPLETED?

TUESDAY	
TASK	COMPLETED?

WEDNESDAY	
TASK	COMPLETED?

THURSDAY	
TASK	COMPLETED?

FRIDAY	
TASK	COMPLETED?

WEEKEND	
TASK	COMPLETED?

Weekly Action Plan

--- WEEK OF ---

MONDAY

TASK	COMPLETED?

TUESDAY

TASK	COMPLETED?

WEDNESDAY

TASK	COMPLETED?

THURSDAY

TASK	COMPLETED?

FRIDAY

TASK	COMPLETED?

WEEKEND

TASK	COMPLETED?

Weekly Action Plan

———— WEEK OF ————

MONDAY

TASK	COMPLETED?

TUESDAY

TASK	COMPLETED?

WEDNESDAY

TASK	COMPLETED?

THURSDAY

TASK	COMPLETED?

FRIDAY

TASK	COMPLETED?

WEEKEND

TASK	COMPLETED?

I release my attachment to things which no longer serve me.

Manifest Journal

My day is full of abundant opportunities and success.

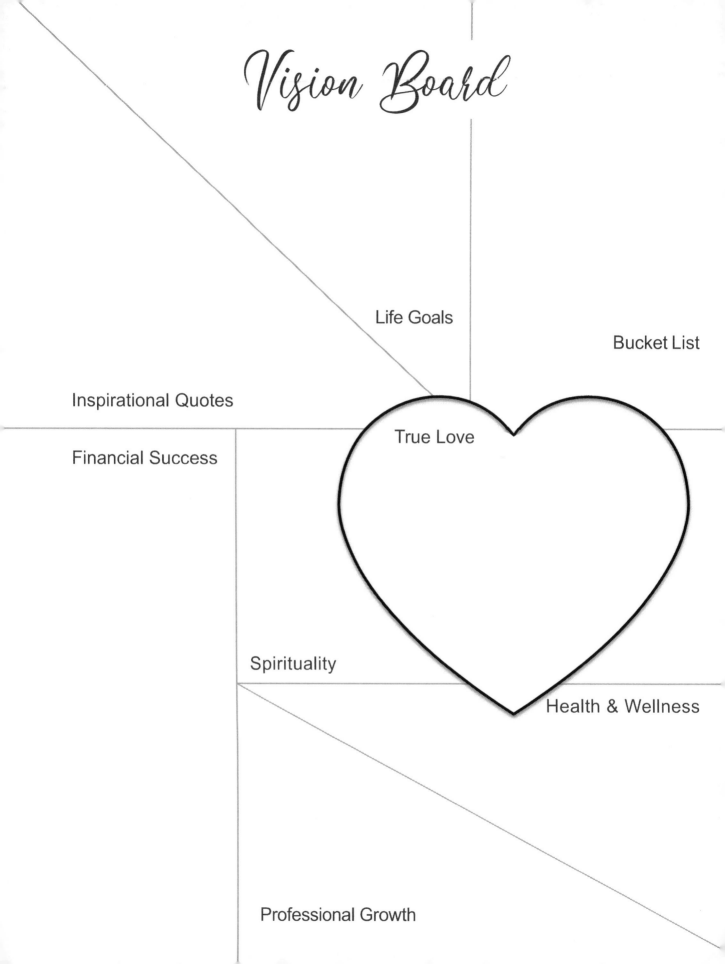

Vision Board

Life Goals

Bucket List

Inspirational Quotes

True Love

Financial Success

Spirituality

Health & Wellness

Professional Growth

Manifest Objective:

_____
_____
_____
_____
_____

Steps to Success

_____
_____
_____
_____
_____
_____
_____
_____
_____
_____

Notes and Reflections

Next New Moon:

_____

Important Dates

_____
_____
_____
_____
_____
_____

Resources

_____
_____
_____
_____
_____

VISION
PLAN
ACTION
SUCCESS

_____
_____
_____
_____
_____

Monthly Planner

MONTH / YEAR

MONDAY	TUESDAY	WEDNESDAY	THURSDAY	FRIDAY	SATURDAY	SUNDAY

Weekly Action Plan

WEEK OF

MONDAY

TASK	COMPLETED?

TUESDAY

TASK	COMPLETED?

WEDNESDAY

TASK	COMPLETED?

THURSDAY

TASK	COMPLETED?

FRIDAY

TASK	COMPLETED?

WEEKEND

TASK	COMPLETED?

Weekly Action Plan

---------------------------------- WEEK OF ----------------------------------

MONDAY

TASK	COMPLETED?

TUESDAY

TASK	COMPLETED?

WEDNESDAY

TASK	COMPLETED?

THURSDAY

TASK	COMPLETED?

FRIDAY

TASK	COMPLETED?

WEEKEND

TASK	COMPLETED?

Weekly Action Plan

WEEK OF

MONDAY

TASK	COMPLETED?

TUESDAY

TASK	COMPLETED?

WEDNESDAY

TASK	COMPLETED?

THURSDAY

TASK	COMPLETED?

FRIDAY

TASK	COMPLETED?

WEEKEND

TASK	COMPLETED?

Weekly Action Plan

———————— WEEK OF ————————

MONDAY

TASK	COMPLETED?

TUESDAY

TASK	COMPLETED?

WEDNESDAY

TASK	COMPLETED?

THURSDAY

TASK	COMPLETED?

FRIDAY

TASK	COMPLETED?

WEEKEND

TASK	COMPLETED?

Weekly Action Plan

WEEK OF

MONDAY	
TASK	COMPLETED?

TUESDAY	
TASK	COMPLETED?

WEDNESDAY	
TASK	COMPLETED?

THURSDAY	
TASK	COMPLETED?

FRIDAY	
TASK	COMPLETED?

WEEKEND	
TASK	COMPLETED?

I attract positive circumstances and positive people into my life.

Date: _____

I appreciate all that I have.

_____

_____

_____

_____

_____

_____

_____

_____

_____

_____

_____

_____

_____

_____

_____

_____

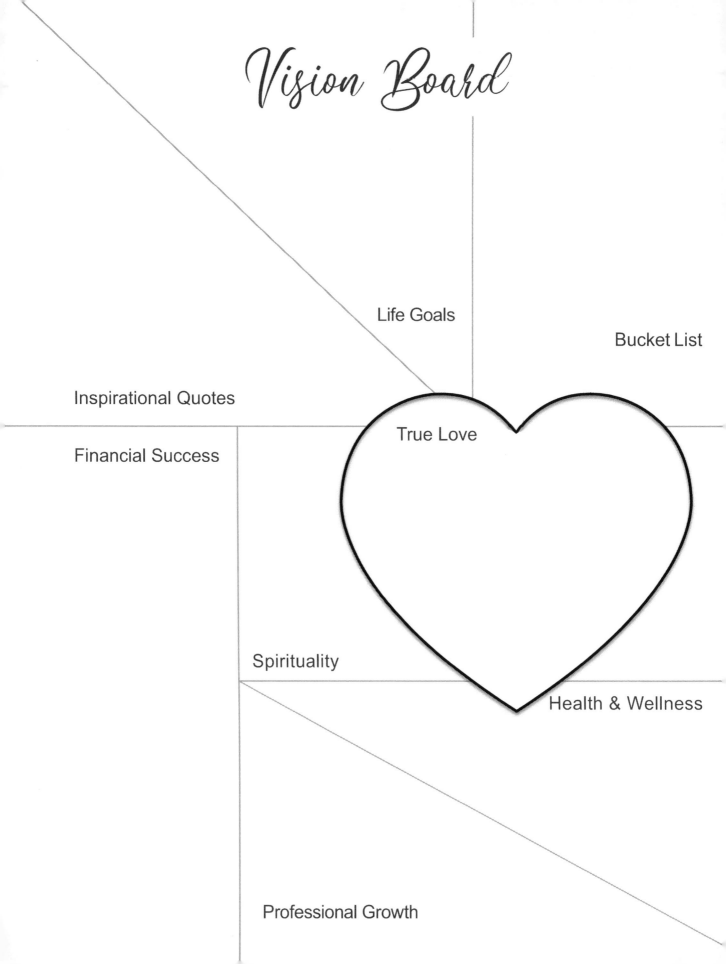

Vision Board

Life Goals

Bucket List

Inspirational Quotes

True Love

Financial Success

Spirituality

Health & Wellness

Professional Growth

Manifest Objective:

_____
_____
_____
_____
_____

Steps to Success

_____
_____
_____
_____
_____
_____
_____
_____
_____
_____
_____
_____
_____

Notes and Reflections

Next New Moon:

_____

Important Dates

_____
_____
_____
_____
_____
_____

Resources

_____
_____
_____
_____
_____
_____

VISION
PLAN
ACTION
SUCCESS

_____
_____
_____
_____
_____

Monthly Planner

MONTH / YEAR

MONDAY	TUESDAY	WEDNESDAY	THURSDAY	FRIDAY	SATURDAY	SUNDAY

Weekly Action Plan

WEEK OF

MONDAY

TASK	COMPLETED?

TUESDAY

TASK	COMPLETED?

WEDNESDAY

TASK	COMPLETED?

THURSDAY

TASK	COMPLETED?

FRIDAY

TASK	COMPLETED?

WEEKEND

TASK	COMPLETED?

Weekly Action Plan

WEEK OF

MONDAY	
TASK	COMPLETED?

TUESDAY	
TASK	COMPLETED?

WEDNESDAY	
TASK	COMPLETED?

THURSDAY	
TASK	COMPLETED?

FRIDAY	
TASK	COMPLETED?

WEEKEND	
TASK	COMPLETED?

Weekly Action Plan

———————— WEEK OF ————————

MONDAY

TASK	COMPLETED?

TUESDAY

TASK	COMPLETED?

WEDNESDAY

TASK	COMPLETED?

THURSDAY

TASK	COMPLETED?

FRIDAY

TASK	COMPLETED?

WEEKEND

TASK	COMPLETED?

Weekly Action Plan

WEEK OF

MONDAY	
TASK	COMPLETED?

TUESDAY	
TASK	COMPLETED?

WEDNESDAY	
TASK	COMPLETED?

THURSDAY	
TASK	COMPLETED?

FRIDAY	
TASK	COMPLETED?

WEEKEND	
TASK	COMPLETED?

Weekly Action Plan

WEEK OF

MONDAY

TASK	COMPLETED?

TUESDAY

TASK	COMPLETED?

WEDNESDAY

TASK	COMPLETED?

THURSDAY

TASK	COMPLETED?

FRIDAY

TASK	COMPLETED?

WEEKEND

TASK	COMPLETED?

Date: _____

The more I love myself, the more love I have to offer.

_____

_____

_____

_____

_____

_____

_____

_____

_____

_____

_____

_____

_____

_____

_____

Date: _____

I begin each day with a grateful heart and open mind.

_____

_____

_____

_____

_____

_____

_____

_____

_____

_____

_____

_____

_____

_____

_____

_____

Manifest Journal

Date: _____

I visualize my ideal life and watch it manifest.

_____

_____

_____

_____

_____

_____

_____

_____

_____

_____

_____

_____

_____

_____

_____

_____

_____

Made in the USA
Middletown, DE
25 September 2023

39238355R00068